Annajanska, the Bolshevik Empress

George Bernard Shaw

Table of Contents

Annajanska, the Bolshevik Empress

George Bernard Shaw

Kessinger Publishing reprints thousands of hard—to—find books!

Visit us at http://www.kessinger.net

160201

Annajanska, the Bolshevik Empress

ANNAJANSKA is frankly a bravura piece. The modern variety theatre demands for its "turns" little plays called sketches, to last twenty minutes or so, and to enable some favorite performer to make a brief but dazzling appearance on some barely passable dramatic pretext. Miss Lillah McCarthy and I, as author and actress, have helped to make one another famous on many serious occasions, from Man and Superman to Androcles; and Mr Charles Ricketts has not disdained to snatch moments from his painting and sculpture to design some wonderful dresses for us. We three unbent as Mrs Siddons, Sir Joshua Reynolds and Dr Johnson might have unbent, to devise a turn for the Coliseum variety theatre. Not that we would set down the art of the variety theatre as something to be condescended to, or our own art as elephantine. We should rather crave indulgence as three novices fresh from the awful legitimacy of the highbrow theatre.

Well, Miss McCarthy and Mr Ricketts justified themselves easily in the glamor of the footlights, to the strains of Tchaikovsky's 1812. I fear I did not. I have received only one compliment on my share; and that was from a friend who said, "It is the only one of your works that is not too long." So I have made it a page or two longer, according to my own precept: EMBRACE YOUR REPROACHES: THEY ARE OFTEN GLORIES IN DISGUISE.

Annajanska was first performed at the Coliseum Theatre in London on the 21st January, 1918, with Lillah McCarthy as the Grand Duchess, Henry Miller as Schneidekind, and Randle Ayrton as General Strammfest.

ANNAJANSKA, THE BOLSHEVIK EMPRESS

The General's office in a military station on the east front in Beotia. An office table with a telephone, writing materials, official papers, etc., is set across the room. At the end of the table, a comfortable chair for the General. Behind the chair, a window. Facing it at the other end of the table, a plain wooden bench. At the side of the table, with its back to the door, a common chair, with a typewriter before it. Beside the door, which is opposite the end of the bench, a rack for caps and coats. There is nobody in the room.

General Strammfest enters, followed by Lieutenant Schneidekind. They hang up their cloaks and caps. Schneidekind takes a little longer than Strammfest, who comes to the table.

STRAMMFEST. Schneidekind.

SCHNEIDEKIND. Yes, sir.

STRAMMFEST. Have you sent my report yet to the government? [He sits down.]

SCHNEIDEKIND [coming to the table]. Not yet, sir. Which government do you wish it sent to? [He sits down.]

STRAMMFEST. That depends. What's the latest? Which of them do you think is most likely to be in power tomorrow morning?

SCHNEIDEKIND. Well, the provisional government was going strong yesterday. But today they say that the Prime Minister has shot himself, and that the extreme left fellow has shot all the others.

STRAMMFEST. Yes: that's all very well; but these fellows always shoot themselves with blank cartridge.

SCHNEIDEKIND. Still, even the blank cartridge means backing down. I should send the report to the Maximilianists.

STRAMMFEST. They're no stronger than the Oppidoshavians; and in my own opinion the Moderate Red Revolutionaries are as likely to come out on top as either of them.

SCHNEIDEKIND. I can easily put a few carbon sheets in the typewriter and send a copy each to the lot.

STRAMMFEST. Waste of paper. You might as well send reports to an infant school. [He throws his head on the table with a groan.]

SCHNEIDEKIND. Tired out, Sir?

STRAMMFEST. O Schneidekind, Schneidekind, how can you bear to live?

SCHNEIDEKIND. At my age, sir, I ask myself how can I bear to die?

STRAMMFEST. You are young, young and heartless. You are excited by the revolution: you are attached to abstract things like liberty. But my family has served the Panjandrums of Beotia faithfully for seven centuries. The Panjandrums have kept our place for us at their courts, honored us, promoted us, shed their glory on us, made us what we are. When I hear you young men declaring that you are fighting for civilization, for democracy, for the overthrow of militarism, I ask myself how can a man shed his blood for empty words used by vulgar tradesmen and common laborers: mere wind and stink. [He rises, exalted by his theme.] A king is a splendid reality, a man raised above us like a god. You can see him; you can kiss his hand; you can be cheered by his smile and terrified by his frown. I would have died for my Panjandrum as my father died for his father. Your toiling millions were only too honored to receive the toes of our boots in the proper spot for them when they displeased their betters. And now what is left in life for me? [He relapses into his chair discouraged.] My Panjandrum is deposed and transported to herd with convicts. The army, his pride and glory, is paraded to hear seditious speeches from penniless rebels, with the colonel actually forced to take the chair and introduce the speaker. I myself am made Commander–in–Chief by my own solicitor: a Jew, Schneidekind! a Hebrew Jew! It seems only yesterday that these things would have been the ravings of a madman: today they are the commonplaces of the gutter press. I live now for three objects only: to defeat the enemy, to restore the Panjandrum, and to hang my solicitor.

SCHNEIDEKIND. Be careful, sir: these are dangerous views to utter nowadays. What if I were to betray you?

STRAMMFEST. What!

SCHNEIDEKIND. I won't, of course: my own father goes on just like that; but suppose I did?

STRAMMFEST [chuckling]. I should accuse you of treason to the Revolution, my lad; and they would immediately shoot you, unless you cried and asked to see your mother before you died, when they would probably change their minds and make you a brigadier. Enough. [He rises and expands his chest.] I feel the better for letting myself go. To business. [He takes up a telegram: opens it: and is thunderstruck by its contents.] Great heaven! [He collapses into his chair. This is the worst blow of all.

SCHNEIDEKIND. What has happened? Are we beaten?

STRAMMFEST. Man, do you think that a mere defeat could strike me down as this news does: I, who have been defeated thirteen times since the war began? O, my master, my master, my Panjandrum! [he is convulsed with sobs.]

SCHNEIDEKIND. They have killed him?

STRAMMFEST. A dagger has been struck through his heart—

SCHNEIDEKIND. Good God!

STRAMMFEST. —and through mine, through mine.

SCHNEIDEKIND [relieved]. Oh, a metaphorical dagger! I thought you meant a real one. What has happened?

STRAMMFEST. His daughter the Grand Duchess Annajanska, she whom the Panjandrina loved beyond all her other children, has—has— [he cannot finish.]

SCHNEIDEKIND. Committed suicide?

STRAMMFEST. No. Better if she had. Oh, far far better.

SCHNEIDEKIND [in hushed tones]. Left the Church?

STRAMMFEST [shocked]. Certainly not. Do not blaspheme, young man.

SCHNEIDEKIND. Asked for the vote?

STRAMMFEST. I would have given it to her with both hands to save her from this.

SCHNEIDEKIND. Save her from what? Dash it, sir, out with it.

STRAMMFEST. She has joined the Revolution.

5

SCHNEIDEKIND. But so have you, sir. We've all joined the Revolution. She doesn't mean it any more than we do.

STRAMMFEST. Heaven grant you may be right! But that is not the worst. She had eloped with a young officer. Eloped, Schneidekind, eloped!

SCHNEIDEKIND [not particularly impressed]. Yes, Sir.

STRAMMFEST. Annajanska, the beautiful, the innocent, my master's daughter! [He buries his face in his hands.]

The telephone rings.

SCHNEIDEKIND [taking the receiver]. Yes: G.H.Q. Yes...Don't bawl: I'm not a general. Who is it speaking?...Why didn't you say so? don't you know your duty? Next time you will lose your stripe...Oh, they've made you a colonel, have they? Well, they've made me a field–marshal: now what have you to say?...Look here: what did you ring up for? I can't spend the day here listening to your cheek...What! the Grand Duchess [Strammfest starts.] Where did you catch her?

STRAMMFEST [snatching the telephone and listening for the answer]. Speak louder, will you: I am a General I know that, you dolt. Have you captured the officer that was with her?... Damnation! You shall answer for this: you let him go: he bribed you. You must have seen him: the fellow is in the full dress court uniform of the Panderobajensky Hussars. I give you twelve hours to catch him or...what's that you say about the devil? Are you swearing at me, you...Thousand thunders! [To Schneidekind.] The swine says that the Grand Duchess is a devil incarnate. [Into the telephone.] Filthy traitor: is that the way you dare speak of the daughter of our anointed Panjandrum? I'll—

SCHNEIDEKIND [pulling the telephone from his lips]. Take care, sir.

STRAMMFEST. I won't take care: I'll have him shot. Let go that telephone.

SCHNEIDEKIND. But for her own sake, sir—

STRAMMFEST. Eh?—

SCHNEIDEKIND. For her own sake they had better send her here. She will be safe in your hands.

STRAMMFEST [yielding the receiver]. You are right. Be civil to him. I should choke [he sits down].

SCHNEIDEKIND [into the telephone]. Hullo. Never mind all that: it's only a fellow here who has been fooling with the telephone. I had to leave the room for a moment. Wash out: and send the girl along. We'll jolly soon teach her to behave herself here...Oh, you've sent her already. Then why the devil didn't you say so, you—[he hangs up the telephone angrily]. Just fancy: they started her off this morning: and all this is because the fellow likes to get on the telephone and hear himself talk now that he is a colonel. [The telephone rings again. He snatches the receiver furiously.] What's the matter now?...[To the General.] It's our own people downstairs. [Into the receiver.] Here! do you suppose I've nothing else to do than to hang on to the telephone all day?...What's that? Not men enough to hold her! What do you mean? [To the General.] She is there, sir.

STRAMMFEST. Tell them to send her up. I shall have to receive her without even rising, without kissing her hand, to keep up appearances before the escort. It will break my heart.

SCHNEIDEKIND [into the receiver]. Send her up...Tcha! [He hangs up the receiver.] He says she is halfway up already: they couldn't hold her.

The Grand Duchess bursts into the room, dragging with her two exhausted soldiers hanging on desperately to her arms. She is enveloped from head to foot by a fur–lined cloak, and wears a fur cap.

SCHNEIDEKIND [pointing to the bench]. At the word Go, place your prisoner on the bench in a sitting posture; and take your seats right and left of her. Go.

The two soldiers make a supreme effort to force her to sit down. She flings them back so that they are forced to sit on the bench to save themselves from falling backwards over it, and is herself dragged into sitting between them. The second soldier, holding on tight to the Grand Duchess with one hand, produces papers with the other, and waves them towards Schneidekind, who takes them from him and passes them on to the General. He

7

opens them and reads them with a grave expression.

SCHNEIDEKIND. Be good enough to wait, prisoner, until the General has read the papers on your case.

THE GRAND DUCHESS [to the soldiers]. Let go. [To Strammfest]. Tell them to let go, or I'll upset the bench backwards and bash our three heads on the floor.

FIRST SOLDIER. No, little mother. Have mercy on the poor.

STRAMMFEST [growling over the edge of the paper he is reading]. Hold your tongue.

THE GRAND DUCHESS [blazing]. Me, or the soldier?

STRAMMFEST [horrified]. The soldier, madam.

THE GRAND DUCHESS. Tell him to let go.

STRAMMFEST. Release the lady.

The soldiers take their hands off her. One of them wipes his fevered brow. The other sucks his wrist.

SCHNEIDEKIND [fiercely]. 'ttention!

The two soldiers sit up stiffly.

THE GRAND DUCHESS. Oh, let the poor man suck his wrist. It may be poisoned. I bit it.

STRAMMFEST [shocked]. You bit a common soldier!

THE GRAND DUCHESS. Well, I offered to cauterize it with the poker in the office stove. But he was afraid. What more could I do?

SCHNEIDEKIND. Why did you bite him, prisoner?

THE GRAND DUCHESS. He would not let go.

STRAMMFEST. Did he let go when you bit him?

THE GRAND DUCHESS. No. [Patting the soldier on the back]. You should give the man a cross for his devotion. I could not go on eating him; so I brought him along with me.

STRAMMFEST. Prisoner—

THE GRAND DUCHESS. Don't call me prisoner, General Strammfest. My grandmother dandled you on her knee.

STRAMMFEST [bursting into tears]. O God, yes. Believe me, my heart is what it was then.

THE GRAND DUCHESS. Your brain also is what it was then. I will not be addressed by you as prisoner.

STRAMMFEST. I may not, for your own sake, call you by your rightful and most sacred titles. What am I to call you?

THE GRAND DUCHESS. The Revolution has made us comrades. Call me comrade.

STRAMMFEST. I had rather die.

THE GRAND DUCHESS. Then call me Annajanska; and I will call you Peter Piper, as grandmamma did.

STRAMMFEST [painfully agitated]. Schneidekind, you must speak to her: I cannot—[he breaks down.]

SCHNEIDEKIND [officially]. The Republic of Beotia has been compelled to confine the Panjandrum and his family, for their own safety, within certain bounds. You have broken those bounds.

STRAMMFEST [taking the word from him]. You are I must say it—a prisoner. What am I to do with you?

THE GRAND DUCHESS. You should have thought of that before you arrested me.

STRAMMFEST. Come, come, prisoner! do you know what will happen to you if you compel me to take a sterner tone with you?

THE GRAND DUCHESS. No. But I know what will happen to you.

STRAMMFEST. Pray what, prisoner?

THE GRAND DUCHESS. Clergyman's sore throat.

Schneidekind splutters; drops a paper: and conceals his laughter under the table.

STRAMMFEST [thunderously]. Lieutenant Schneidekind.

SCHNEIDEKIND [in a stifled voice]. Yes, Sir. [The table vibrates visibly.]

STRAMMFEST. Come out of it, you fool: you're upsetting the ink.

Schneidekind emerges, red in the face with suppressed mirth.

STRAMMFEST. Why don't you laugh? Don't you appreciate Her Imperial Highness's joke?

SCHNEIDEKIND [suddenly becoming solemn]. I don't want to, sir.

STRAMMFEST. Laugh at once, sir. I order you to laugh.

SCHNEIDEKIND [with a touch of temper]. I really can't, sir. [He sits down decisively.]

STRAMMFEST [growling at him]. Yah! [He turns impressively to the Grand Duchess.] Your Imperial Highness desires me to address you as comrade?

THE GRAND DUCHESS [rising and waving a red handkerchief]. Long live the Revolution, comrade!

STRAMMFEST [rising and saluting]. Proletarians of all lands, unite. Lieutenant Schneidekind, you will rise and sing the Marseillaise.

SCHNEIDEKIND [rising]. But I cannot, sir. I have no voice, no ear.

STRAMMFEST. Then sit down; and bury your shame in your typewriter. [Schneidekind sits down.] Comrade Annajanska, you have eloped with a young officer.

THE GRAND DUCHESS [astounded]. General Strammfest, you lie.

STRAMMFEST. Denial, comrade, is useless. It is through that officer that your movements have been traced. [The Grand Duchess is suddenly enlightened, and seems amused. Strammfest continues an a forensic manner.] He joined you at the Golden Anchor in Hakonsburg. You gave us the slip there; but the officer was traced to Potterdam, where you rejoined him and went alone to Premsylople. What have you done with that unhappy young man? Where is he?

THE GRAND DUCHESS [pretending to whisper an important secret]. Where he has always been.

STRAMMFEST [eagerly]. Where is that?

THE GRAND DUCHESS [impetuously]. In your imagination. I came alone. I am alone. Hundreds of officers travel every day from Hakonsburg to Potterdam. What do I know about them?

STRAMMFEST. They travel in khaki. They do not travel in full dress court uniform as this man did.

SCHNEIDEKIND. Only officers who are eloping with grand duchesses wear court uniform: otherwise the grand duchesses could not be seen with them.

STRAMMFEST. Hold your tongue. [Schneidekind, in high dudgeon, folds his arms and retires from the conversation. The General returns to his paper and to his examination of the Grand Duchess.] This officer travelled with your passport. What have you to say to that?

THE GRAND DUCHESS. Bosh! How could a man travel with a woman's passport?

STRAMMFEST. It is quite simple, as you very well know. A dozen travellers arrive at the boundary. The official collects their passports. He counts twelve persons; then counts the passports. If there are twelve, he is satisfied.

THE GRAND DUCHESS. Then how do you know that one of the passports was mine?

STRAMMFEST. A waiter at the Potterdam Hotel looked at the officer's passport when he was in his bath. It was your passport.

THE GRAND DUCHESS. Stuff! Why did he not have me arrested?

STRAMMFEST. When the waiter returned to the hotel with the police the officer had vanished; and you were there with your own passport. They knouted him.

THE GRAND DUCHESS. Oh! Strammfest, send these men away. I must speak to you alone.

STRAMMFEST [rising in horror]. No: this is the last straw: I cannot consent. It is impossible, utterly, eternally impossible, that a daughter of the Imperial House should speak to any one alone, were it even her own husband.

THE GRAND DUCHESS. You forget that there is an exception. She may speak to a child alone. [She rises.] Strammfest, you have been dandled on my grandmother's knee. By that gracious action the dowager Panjandrina made you a child forever. So did Nature, by the way. I order you to speak to me alone. Do you hear? I order you. For seven hundred years no member of your family has ever disobeyed an order from a member of mine. Will you disobey me?

STRAMMFEST. There is an alternative to obedience. The dead cannot disobey. [He takes out his pistol and places the muzzle against his temple.]

SCHNEIDEKIND [snatching the pistol from him]. For God's sake, General—

STRAMMFEST [attacking him furiously to recover the weapon]. Dog of a subaltern, restore that pistol and my honor.

SCHNEIDEKIND [reaching out with the pistol to the Grand Duchess]. Take it: quick: he is as strong as a bull.

THE GRAND DUCHESS [snatching it]. Aha! Leave the room, all of you except the General. At the double! lightning! electricity! [She fires shot after shot, spattering the bullets about the ankles of the soldiers. They fly precipitately. She turns to Schneidekind, who has by this time been flung on the floor by the General.] You too. [He scrambles up.] March. [He flies to the door.]

SCHNEIDEKIND [turning at the door]. For your own sake, comrade—

THE GRAND DUCHESS [indignantly]. Comrade! You!!! Go. [She fires two more shots. He vanishes.]

STRAMMFEST [making an impulsive movement towards her]. My Imperial Mistress—

THE GRAND DUCHESS. Stop. I have one bullet left, if you attempt to take this from me [putting the pistol to her temple].

STRAMMFEST [recoiling, and covering his eyes with his hands]. No no: put it down: put it down. I promise everything: I swear anything; but put it down, I implore you.

THE GRAND DUCHESS [throwing it on the table]. There!

STRAMMFEST [uncovering his eyes]. Thank God!

THE GRAND DUCHESS [gently]. Strammfest: I am your comrade. Am I nothing more to you?

STRAMMFEST [falling on his knee]. You are, God help me, all that is left to me of the only power I recognize on earth [he kisses her hand].

THE GRAND DUCHESS [indulgently]. Idolater! When will you learn that our strength has never been in ourselves, but in your illusions about us? [She shakes off her kindliness, and sits down in his chair.] Now tell me, what are your orders? And do you mean to obey them?

STRAMMFEST [starting like a goaded ox, and blundering fretfully about the room]. How can I obey six different dictators, and not one gentleman among the lot of them? One of them orders me to make peace with the foreign enemy. Another orders me to offer all the neutral countries 48 hours to choose between adopting his views on the single tax and being instantly invaded and annihilated. A third orders me to go to a damned Socialist Conference and explain that Beotia will allow no annexations and no indemnities, and merely wishes to establish the Kingdom of Heaven on Earth throughout the universe. [He finishes behind Schneidekind's chair.]

THE GRAND DUCHESS. Damn their trifling!

STRAMMFEST. I thank Your Imperial Highness from the bottom of my heart for that expression. Europe thanks you.

THE GRAND DUCHESS. M'yes; but—[rising]. Strammfest, you know that your cause—the cause of the dynasty—is lost.

STRAMMFEST. You must not say so. It is treason, even from you. [He sinks, discouraged, into the chair, and covers his face with his hand.]

THE GRAND DUCHESS. Do not deceive yourself, General: never again will a Panjandrum reign in Beotia. [She walks slowly across the room, brooding bitterly, and thinking aloud.] We are so decayed, so out of date, so feeble, so wicked in our own despite, that we have come at last to will our own destruction.

STRAMMFEST. You are uttering blasphemy.

THE GRAND DUCHESS. All great truths begin as blasphemies. All the king's horses and all the king's men cannot set up my father's throne again. If they could, you would have done it, would you not?

STRAMMFEST. God knows I would!

THE GRAND DUCHESS. You really mean that? You would keep the people in their hopeless squalid misery? you would fill those infamous prisons again with the noblest spirits in the land? you would thrust the rising sun of liberty back into the sea of blood from which it has risen? And all because there was in the middle of the dirt and ugliness and horror a little patch of court splendor in which you could stand with a few orders on your uniform, and yawn day after day and night after night in unspeakable boredom until your grave yawned wider still, and you fell into it because you had nothing better to do. How can you be so stupid, so heartless?

STRAMMFEST. You must be mad to think of royalty in such a way. I never yawned at court. The dogs yawned; but that was because they were dogs: they had no imagination, no ideals, no sense of honor and dignity to sustain them.

THE GRAND DUCHESS. My poor Strammfest: you were not often enough at court to tire of it. You were mostly soldiering; and when you came home to have a new order pinned on your breast, your happiness came through looking at my father and mother and at me, and adoring us. Was that not so?

STRAMMFEST. Do YOU reproach me with it? I am not ashamed of it.

THE GRAND DUCHESS. Oh, it was all very well for you, Strammfest. But think of me, of me! standing there for you to gape at, and knowing that I was no goddess, but only a girl like any other girl! It was cruelty to animals: you could have stuck up a wax doll or a golden calf to worship; it would not have been bored.

STRAMMFEST. Stop; or I shall renounce my allegiance to you. I have had women flogged for such seditious chatter as this.

THE GRAND DUCHESS. Do not provoke me to send a bullet through your head for reminding me of it.

15

Annajanska, the Bolshevik Empress

STRAMMFEST. You always had low tastes. You are no true daughter of the Panjandrums: you are a changeling, thrust into the Panjandrina's bed by some profligate nurse. I have heard stories of your childhood: of how—

THE GRAND DUCHESS. Ha, ha! Yes: they took me to the circus when I was a child. It was my first moment of happiness, my first glimpse of heaven. I ran away and joined the troupe. They caught me and dragged me back to my gilded cage; but I had tasted freedom; and they never could make me forget it.

STRAMMFEST. Freedom! To be the slave of an acrobat! to be exhibited to the public! to—

THE GRAND DUCHESS. Oh, I was trained to that. I had learnt that part of the business at court.

STRAMMFEST. You had not been taught to strip yourself half naked and turn head over heels—

THE GRAND DUCHESS. Man, I WANTED to get rid of my swaddling clothes and turn head over heels. I wanted to, I wanted to, I wanted to. I can do it still. Shall I do it now?

STRAMMFEST. If you do, I swear I will throw myself from the window so that I may meet your parents in heaven without having my medals torn from my breast by them.

THE GRAND DUCHESS. Oh, you are incorrigible. You are mad, infatuated. You will not believe that we royal divinities are mere common flesh and blood even when we step down from our pedestals and tell you ourselves what a fool you are. I will argue no more with you: I will use my power. At a word from me your men will turn against you: already half of them do not salute you; and you dare not punish them: you have to pretend not to notice it.

STRAMMFEST. It is not for you to taunt me with that if it is so.

THE GRAND DUCHESS. [haughtily]. Taunt! I condescend to taunt! To taunt a common General! You forget yourself, sir.

STRAMMFEST [dropping on his knee submissively]. Now at last you speak like your royal self.

THE GRAND DUCHESS. Oh, Strammfest, Strammfest, they have driven your slavery into your very bones. Why did you not spit in my face?.

STRAMMFEST [rising with a shudder]. God forbid!

THE GRAND DUCHESS. Well, since you will be my slave, take your orders from me. I have not come here to save our wretched family and our bloodstained crown. I am come to save the Revolution.

STRAMMFEST. Stupid as I am, I have come to think that I had better save that than save nothing. But what will the Revolution do for the people? Do not be deceived by the fine speeches of the revolutionary leaders and the pamphlets of the revolutionary writers. How much liberty is there where they have gained the upper hand? Are they not hanging, shooting, imprisoning as much as ever we did? Do they ever tell the people the truth? No: if the truth does not suit them they spread lies instead, and make it a crime to tell the truth.

THE GRAND DUCHESS. Of course they do. Why should they not?

STRAMMFEST [hardly able to believe his ears]. Why should they not?

THE GRAND DUCHESS. Yes: why should they not? We did it. You did it, whip in hand: you flogged women for teaching children to read.

STRAMMFEST. To read sedition. To read Karl Marx.

THE GRAND DUCHESS. Pshaw! How could they learn to read the Bible without learning to read Karl Marx? Why do you not stand to your guns and justify what you did, instead of making silly excuses? Do you suppose I think flogging a woman worse than flogging a man? I, who am a woman myself!

STRAMMFEST. I am at a loss to understand your Imperial Highness. You seem to me to contradict yourself.

THE GRAND DUCHESS. Nonsense! I say that if the people cannot govern themselves, they must be governed by somebody. If they will not do their duty without being half forced and half humbugged, somebody must force them and humbug them. Some energetic and capable minority must always be in power. Well, I am on the side of the energetic minority whose principles I agree with. The Revolution is as cruel as we were; but its aims are my aims. Therefore I stand for the Revolution.

STRAMMFEST. You do not know what you are saying. This is pure Bolshevism. Are you, the daughter of a Panjandrum, a Bolshevist?

THE GRAND DUCHESS. I am anything that will make the world less like a prison and more like a circus.

STRAMMFEST. Ah! You still want to be a circus star.

THE GRAND DUCHESS. Yes, and be billed as the Bolshevik Empress. Nothing shall stop me. You have your orders, General Strammfest: save the Revolution.

STRAMMFEST. What Revolution? Which Revolution? No two of your rabble of revolutionists mean the same thing by the Revolution What can save a mob in which every man is rushing in a different direction?

THE GRAND DUCHESS. I will tell you. The war can save it.

STRAMMFEST. The war?

THE GRAND DUCHESS. Yes, the war. Only a great common danger and a great common duty can unite us and weld these wrangling factions into a solid commonwealth.

STRAMMFEST. Bravo! War sets everything right: I have always said so. But what is a united people without a united army? And what can I do? I am only a soldier. I cannot make speeches: I have won no victories: they will not rally to my call [again he sinks into his chair with his former gesture of discouragement].

THE GRAND DUCHESS. Are you sure they will not rally to mine?

STRAMMFEST. Oh, if only you were a man and a soldier!

THE GRAND DUCHESS. Suppose I find you a man and a soldier?

STRAMMFEST [rising in a fury]. Ah! the scoundrel you eloped with! You think you will shove this fellow into an army command, over my head. Never.

THE GRAND DUCHESS. You promised everything. You swore anything. [She marches as if in front of a regiment.] I know that this man alone can rouse the army to enthusiasm.

STRAMMFEST. Delusion! Folly! He is some circus acrobat; and you are in love with him.

THE GRAND DUCHESS. I swear I am not in love with him. I swear I will never marry him.

STRAMMFEST. Then who is he?

THE GRAND DUCHESS. Anybody in the world but you would have guessed long ago. He is under your very eyes.

STRAMMFEST [staring past her right and left]. Where?

THE GRAND DUCHESS. Look out of the window.

He rushes to the window, looking for the officer. The Grand Duchess takes off her cloak and appears in the uniform of the Panderobajensky Hussars.

STRAMMFEST [peering through the window]. Where is he? I can see no one.

THE GRAND DUCHESS. Here, silly.

STRAMMFEST [turning]. You! Great Heavens! The Bolshevik Empress!

Printed in the United States
219414BV00003B/33/A

9 781419 107108